HELLO
MY NAME IS

YOUR BEST YEAR: 2014 WORKBOOK & PLANNER

BY LISA JACOBS

LIFE: LIVE IT, LOVE IT

I have an important request of everyone who reads this series. I ask it kindly, but urgently: please do not compromise with this life. Please do not vaguely wish for more money, more exposure, more family time, more love, more success, more laughter, or more adventure. If you want more of anything, turn off the TV or stop surfing the internet, sit down with yourself, and clearly identify what needs to change for you to feel fulfilled, satisfied, and hungry for more Life every day!

BECAUSE WE ALL DESERVE MORE LIFE! IN OUR LIFE.

This means no more accepting, keeping, or doing what you don't want. It's a tough statement because it calls for change. Change can be uncomfortable - but the discomfort only lasts a minute in the grand scheme of things.

As Cherie Carter-Scott said, "You deserve to have everything in your life exactly as you want it." To kick-start your best year ever, I ask that you write a list of the 25 things you want most in this life ...

··· 25 TOP GOALS ···

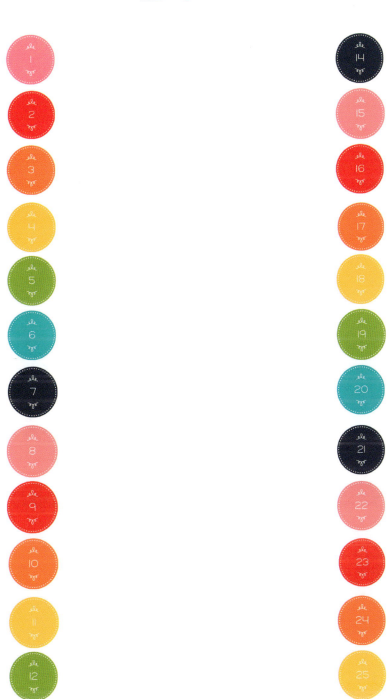

Next, look back on those goals you just listed and circle the 5 that matter more than anything else.

CLEAR PRIORITIES + FOCUS = DREAMS COME TRUE

Those top 5 goals that you circled are the goals you're going to focus on in the coming year. Let's call them your "intentions." They're the most pressing, and if you look closer, they're probably the key to unlocking all of the other dreams and desires you have.

As you plan the coming year, be sure that your to-do list brings you the results you want toward the goals you prioritize. And remember: keep your goals challenging, yet doable. They should make you feel good and excited, NOT anxiety-ridden.

"YOU SHOULD USE THE SAME TECHNIQUES IN [GOAL-SETTING] THAT JACKIE BURKE RECOMMENDS IN PUTTING. THAT IS, NOT TO FEEL THAT YOU HAVE TO PINPOINT THE BALL RIGHT TO THE CUP ITSELF ON A LONG PUTT, BUT TO AIM AT AN AREA THE SIZE OF A WASHTUB. THIS TAKES OFF THE STRAIN, RELAXES YOU, ENABLES YOU TO PERFORM BETTER. IF IT'S GOOD ENOUGH FOR THE PROFESSIONALS, IT SHOULD BE GOOD ENOUGH FOR YOU."

–MAXWELL MALTZ

2014 TOP 5 INTENTIONS

ONE

TWO

THREE

FOUR

FIVE

CREATIVE CONNECTIONS

LIST AT LEAST 20 PEOPLE TO SUPPORT,
COLLABORATE WITH, MENTOR, INTERVIEW,
INTRODUCE YOURSELF TO, OR SIMPLY ADMIRE ....

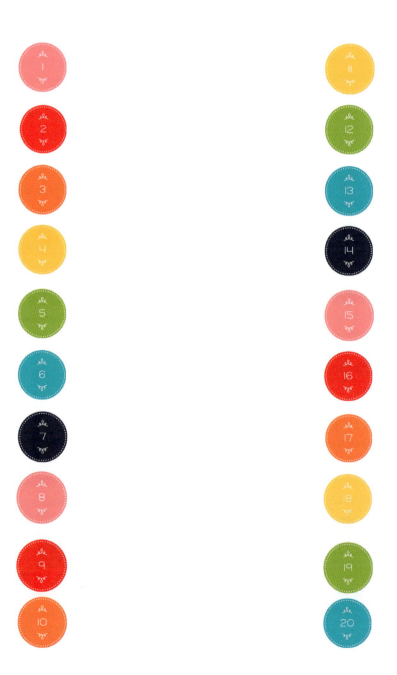

1
2
3
4
5
6
7
8
9
10

11
12
13
14
15
16
17
18
19
20

··· JOURNAL PROMPTS ···

DREAM *BIG* AND FILL IN THE BLANKS BELOW!

_____ CALLS ME.

I BUILD _____.

I EARN _____.

I'M OFFERED _____.

_____ FEATURES MY WORK.

I FEEL _____.

I DON'T HAVE TO WORRY ABOUT _____

_____ ANYMORE.

I HAVE PLENTY OF _____.

THE PEOPLE IN MY LIFE ADD _____.

HOW TO GET TO WHERE
❧ YOU WANT TO BE ❧

Going forward, short-term, long-term, and annual goals will be essential to your success. You've established a list of 25 long-term goals, and now it's time to work on short-term and annual goals to see them through.

Keep your top 5 intentions handy; they're important! Your short-term and annual goals will be generated by honoring those intentions and determining what you need to do to move toward making your dreams come true. It's that simple!

TAKE SMALL STEPS TOWARD YOUR GOALS EVERY DAY.

How do you get from where you are to where you want to be? You physically move toward it. If you wanted to travel from Pittsburgh to New York, you can't sit down on a park bench in Pittsburgh and wonder why you're not getting to New York.

It seems too simple to be true, but few people actively move toward their dreams. Most people are sitting on a park bench complaining about how their dreams aren't showing up for them. Can New York show up in Pittsburgh? No!

Over the next few pages, you'll be prompted to figure out what is working in your life so that you can focus on doing a whole lot more of that. This will help you determine how to get from where you're at to where you want to be and eliminate time-wasting tasks and busywork.

WHAT'S WORKING?

What activities, products, actions, or ideas worked for you this year?

What was your best creative business payday? What product or services sold well? What actions brought subscribers, fans and followers?

(If there are none, don't worry! But take note. Going forward, you'll want to focus your efforts on activities that DO generate these results.)

What didn't work? What's costing time and money without generating a return?

What do you want MORE of in 2014?

How might you change your approach going forward?

THE COLD HARD FACTS

Boom. Take a few minutes to gather up your data and exact numbers, and write down the following:

How many subscribers do you have on your email list?

Gross profit: How much did your business earn in 2013 (to date)?

Expenses: What were your total expenses in 2013 (to date)?

$$GROSS\ PROFIT - EXPENSES = NET\ PROFIT$$

Net profit: What is your net profit (to date) in 2013?

(Again, If there is no profit, don't worry! But take note. Going forward, you'll want to focus your efforts on activities that DO generate these results.)

In what ways has your business grown in 2013? And, how would you like it to grow in the coming year?

WHY AREN'T YOU RICH YET?

In one of my favorite books of the year, The Instant Millionaire: A Tale of Wisdom and Wealth, a wise old millionaire asks a struggling young man, "How is it that you aren't rich yet? Have you ever seriously asked yourself that question?"

This reminds me of productivity and how we're too often planning our next move rather than taking it! Here are some time management questions to ponder:

When you <u>don't</u> want to do something, what do you do instead?

How many piles of unfinished paperwork, projects, and resources do you have lying around? What would it take to finish or organize them?

After you finish your current project, do you typically know what you'll work on next? And if not, why not?

❧ LET'S TALK TURKEY ❧

What amount of money could you earn in 2014 that would leave you feeling abundant, secure, wealthy, FREE, peaceful, confident, and assured? Write down an exact number here:

From that amount, name the top 5 items, products and/or lifestyle changes you would like to spend some of your profits on:

THE MONEY PAGE

How many subscribers/friends/followers do you want to have by December 31, 2014?

List at least 10 things you're going to try (or regularly do, if it's working) to make that happen. Estimate the number of subscribers each action will bring:

How much money (net profit) would you like to make by December 31, 2014?

List at least 10 actions you're going to take (and regularly do, if it's working) to make that happen. Estimate the amount of money each action will make:

WHAT DOES SUCCESS LOOK LIKE TO YOU?

How will you know if you arrived if you don't know what the destination looks like? Create your own definition of success by filling out the following prompts. When you become very successful ...

What good things do you have a whole lot more of in your life?

How much money have you earned? How prosperous do you feel?

How healthy are you? What do you look like?

What (or whom) do you release that's no longer working in your life?

What had you been holding onto that was holding you back?

What has to happen by the end of 2014 in order for the year to feel like an absolute success?

HOW TO GET THE
❧ RESULTS YOU WANT ❧

To get the results you want, you must name the specific actions you can take to generate those results, and then give yourself a deadline to get those actions accomplished. With proper planning, the actions you list will help you close the gap between where you are now and where you want to be by this time next year. Examples are:

- Encourage 100 customers to join my email list.
- Plan promotions six months ahead of time.
- Build a specific amount of stock.
- Launch a new product line.
- Write a book or e-program.
- Start a blog.
- Streamline my process to increase productivity.
- Find 50 new customers.

I recommend deadlines of 6 months or less. After you've determined a challenging, yet doable timeframe, name the date.

For example, if I choose six-month's worth of actions in December, I would fill in the following page with the above tasks and a deadline, like this:

I ACCOMPLISH THESE TASKS BY:

June 30, 2014

If you are new to this type of goal-planning, create a list for no more than 3 months in advance. With practice, you'll have a better understanding of how much you can realistically accomplish in larger timeframes. Find extra copies of this worksheet at marketyourcreativity.com.

❧ THE RESULTS I WANT ❦

I ACCOMPLISH THESE TASKS BY:

MONEY AFFIRMATIONS!
(BY LOUISE HAY)

♡ MY INCOME IS CONSTANTLY INCREASING. ♡

♡ I PROSPER WHEREVER I TURN. ♡

♡ TODAY IS A DELIGHTFUL DAY. MONEY COMES TO ME IN EXPECTED AND UNEXPECTED WAYS. ♡

♡ I GIVE MYSELF THE GREEN LIGHT TO GO AHEAD, AND TO JOYOUSLY EMBRACE THE NEW. ♡

♡ I SUPPORT OTHERS IN BECOMING PROSPEROUS, AND IN TURN, LIFE SUPPORTS ME IN WONDROUS WAYS. ♡

♡ I AM NOW WILLING TO BE OPEN TO THE UNLIMITED PROSPERITY THAT EXISTS EVERYWHERE. ♡

♡ I LIVE IN A LOVING, ABUNDANT, HARMONIOUS UNIVERSE, AND I AM GRATEFUL. ♡

♡ I DESERVE THE BEST, AND I ACCEPT THE BEST NOW. ♡

♡ ALL IS WELL, AND I AM SAFE. ♡

FIND MORE INSPIRATION BY FOLLOWING LOUISE HAY ON FACEBOOK AT:
HTTPS://WWW.FACEBOOK.COM/LOUISELHAY

14 BEFORE 2014

Before you launch into creating your 14 Before 2014 (14 goals you want to accomplish BEFORE the New Year), look back over your list of 25 goals and top 5 intentions.

What do you need to clear out of the way before you can really get down to business on your best year goals?

What unfinished business do you need to attend to so that you can start the New Year with a clean slate?

What do you need to research or learn before making your goals happen?

What projects do you have to let go of? What commitments might you need to say "no" to?

What people, activities, and events do you want to really enjoy and be present for during this time?

14 BEFORE 2014

1.

2.

3.

4.

5.

6.

7.

8.

9.

10.

11.

12.

13.

14.

TO ACCOMPLISH IN ...

OCTOBER

1
2
3
4
5
6
7
8
9
10
11
12
13
14
15
16
17
18
19
20
21
22
23
24
25
26
27
28
29
30
31

❧LIVE FREE : LOVE LIFE❧

NOVEMBER

1
2
3
4
5
6
7
8
9
10
11
12
13
14
15
16
17
18
19
20
21
22
23
24
25
26
27
28
29
30

❧LIVE FREE : LOVE LIFE❧

2 0 1 3

TO ACCOMPLISH IN ..

DECEMBER

1
2
3
4
5
6
7
8
9
10
11
12
13
14
15
16
17
18
19
20
21
22
23
24
25
26
27
28
29
30
31

❧LIVE FREE : LOVE LIFE❧

2013

NOTES

❧LIVE FREE : LOVE LIFE❧

✕✕✕✕✕✕✕ OCTOBER 2013 ✕✕✕✕✕✕✕

SUNDAY	MONDAY	TUESDAY	WEDNESDAY	THURSDAY	FRIDAY	SATURDAY
		1	2	3	4	5
6	7	8	9	10	11	12
13	14	15	16	17	18	19
20	21	22	23	24	25	26
27	28	29	30	31		

SEPTEMBER 2013
S	M	T	W	T	F	S
1	2	3	4	5	6	7
8	9	10	11	12	13	14
15	16	17	18	19	20	21
22	23	24	25	26	27	28
29	30					

NOVEMBER 2013
S	M	T	W	T	F	S
					1	2
3	4	5	6	7	8	9
10	11	12	13	14	15	16
17	18	19	20	21	22	23
24	25	26	27	28	29	30

NOTES:

TO-DO IN ... OCTOBER

MUST-DO THIS WEEK:

1.

2.

3.

OCT

2013

30

1

2

NOTES

OCT

2013

3

4

5

6

MUST-DO THIS WEEK:

1.

2.

3.

OCT

2013

7

8

9

NOTES

OCT

2013

10

11

12

13

MUST-DO THIS WEEK:

1.
2.
3.

OCT

2013

14

15

16

NOTES

OCT

2013

17

18

19

20

MUST-DO THIS WEEK:

1.

2.

3.

OCT

2013

21

22

23

NOTES

OCT

2013

24

25

26

27

MUST-DO THIS WEEK:

1.

2.

3.

OCT

2013

28

29

30

NOTES

OCT

2013

31

NOV

1

2

3

NOVEMBER 2013

SUNDAY	MONDAY	TUESDAY	WEDNESDAY	THURSDAY	FRIDAY	SATURDAY
OCTOBER 2013 / DECEMBER 2013					1	2
3	4	5	6	7	8	9
10	11	12	13	14	15	16
17	18	19	20	21	22	23
24	25	26	27	28	29	30

OCTOBER 2013
S M T W T F S
      1 2 3 4 5
6 7 8 9 10 11 12
13 14 15 16 17 18 19
20 21 22 23 24 25 26
27 28 29 30 31

DECEMBER 2013
S M T W T F S
1 2 3 4 5 6 7
8 9 10 11 12 13 14
15 16 17 18 19 20 21
22 23 24 25 26 27 28
29 30 31

NOTES:

MUST-DO THIS WEEK:

1.
2.
3.

NOV

2013

4

5

6

NOTES

NOV

2013

7

8

9

10

MUST-DO THIS WEEK:

1.

2.

3.

NOV

2013

11

12

13

NOTES

NOV

2013

14

15

16

17

MUST-DO THIS WEEK:

1.
2.
3.

NOV
2013

18

19

20

NOTES

NOV

2013

21

22

23

24

MUST-DO THIS WEEK:

1.

2.

3.

NOV

2013

25

26

27

NOTES

NOV
2013

28

29

30

DEC

1

DECEMBER 2013

SUNDAY	MONDAY	TUESDAY	WEDNESDAY	THURSDAY	FRIDAY	SATURDAY
1	2	3	4	5	6	7
8	9	10	11	12	13	14
15	16	17	18	19	20	21
22	23	24	25	26	27	28
29	30	31				

NOVEMBER 2013
S	M	T	W	T	F	S
					1	2
3	4	5	6	7	8	9
10	11	12	13	14	15	16
17	18	19	20	21	22	23
24	25	26	27	28	29	30

JANUARY 2014
S	M	T	W	T	F	S
			1	2	3	4
5	6	7	8	9	10	11
12	13	14	15	16	17	18
19	20	21	22	23	24	25
26	27	28	29	30	31	

NOTES:

TO-DO IN ... DECEMBER

MUST-DO THIS WEEK:

1.

2.

3.

DEC

2013

2

3

4

NOTES

DEC

2013

5

6

7

8

MUST-DO THIS WEEK:

1.

2.

3.

DEC

2013

9

10

11

NOTES

DEC

2013

12

13

14

15

MUST-DO THIS WEEK:

1.
2.
3.

DEC

2013

16

17

18

NOTES

DEC

2013

19

20

21

22

MUST-DO THIS WEEK:

1.

2.

3.

DEC

2013

23

24

25

NOTES

DEC
2013

26

27

28

29

MUST-DO THIS WEEK:

1.

2.

3.

DEC

2013

30

31

JAN

1

NOTES

HAPPY NEW YEAR

2014 RESOLUTIONS

TO ACCOMPLISH IN ...

JANUARY

1
2
3
4
5
6
7
8
9
10
11
12
13
14
15
16
17
18
19
20
21
22
23
24
25
26
27
28
29
30
31

LIVE FREE : LOVE LIFE

FEBRUARY

1
2
3
4
5
6
7
8
9
10
11
12
13
14
15
16
17
18
19
20
21
22
23
24
25
26
27
28

LIVE FREE : LOVE LIFE

2014

TO ACCOMPLISH IN ...

MARCH

1
2
3
4
5
6
7
8
9
10
11
12
13
14
15
16
17
18
19
20
21
22
23
24
25
26
27
28
29
30
31

LIVE FREE : LOVE LIFE

2014

NOTES

LIVE FREE : LOVE LIFE

JANUARY 2014

SUNDAY	MONDAY	TUESDAY	WEDNESDAY	THURSDAY	FRIDAY	SATURDAY
			1	2	3	4
5	6	7	8	9	10	11
12	13	14	15	16	17	18
19	20	21	22	23	24	25
26	27	28	29	30	31	

DECEMBER 2013

S	M	T	W	T	F	S
1	2	3	4	5	6	7
8	9	10	11	12	13	14
15	16	17	18	19	20	21
22	23	24	25	26	27	28
29	30	31				

FEBRUARY 2014

S	M	T	W	T	F	S
						1
2	3	4	5	6	7	8
9	10	11	12	13	14	15
16	17	18	19	20	21	22
23	24	25	26	27	28	

NOTES:

TO-DO IN ... JANUARY

JAN

2014

2

3

4

5

MUST-DO THIS WEEK:

1.

2.

3.

JAN

2014

6

7

8

NOTES

JAN

2014

9

10

11

12

MUST-DO THIS WEEK:

1.
2.
3.

JAN

2014

13

14

15

NOTES

JAN

2014

16

17

18

19

MUST-DO THIS WEEK:

1.

2.

3.

JAN

2014

20

21

22

NOTES

JAN

2014

23

24

25

26

MUST-DO THIS WEEK:

1.

2.

3.

JAN

2014

27

28

29

NOTES

JAN

2014

30

31

FEB

1

2

FEBRUARY 2014

SUNDAY	MONDAY	TUESDAY	WEDNESDAY	THURSDAY	FRIDAY	SATURDAY
JANUARY 2014 S M T W T F S 1 2 3 4 5 6 7 8 9 10 11 12 13 14 15 16 17 18 19 20 21 22 23 24 25 26 27 28 29 30 31	**MARCH 2014** S M T W T F S 1 2 3 4 5 6 7 8 9 10 11 12 13 14 15 16 17 18 19 20 21 22 23 24 25 26 27 28 29					1
2	3	4	5	6	7	8
9	10	11	12	13	14	15
16	17	18	19	20	21	22
23	24	25	26	27	28	

NOTES:

TO-DO IN ... FEBRUARY

MUST-DO THIS WEEK:

1.

2.

3.

FEB

2014

3

4

5

NOTES

FEB

2014

6

7

8

9

MUST-DO THIS WEEK:

1.

2.

3.

FEB

2014

10

11

12

NOTES

FEB

2014

13

14

15

16

MUST-DO THIS WEEK:

1.

2.

3.

FEB

2014

17

18

19

NOTES

FEB

2014

20

21

22

23

MUST-DO THIS WEEK:

1.
2.
3.

FEB

2014

24

25

26

NOTES

FEB

2014

27

28

MAR

1

2

MARCH 2014

SUNDAY	MONDAY	TUESDAY	WEDNESDAY	THURSDAY	FRIDAY	SATURDAY
2	3	4	5	6	7	8
9	10	11	12	13	14	15
16	17	18	19	20	21	22
23	24					
30	31	25	26	27	28	29

FEBRUARY 2014

S	M	T	W	T	F	S
						1
2	3	4	5	6	7	8
9	10	11	12	13	14	15
16	17	18	19	20	21	22
23	24	25	26	27	28	

APRIL 2014

S	M	T	W	T	F	S
		1	2	3	4	5
6	7	8	9	10	11	12
13	14	15	16	17	18	19
20	21	22	23	24	25	26
27	28	29	30			

NOTES:

TO-DO IN ...   MARCH

MUST-DO THIS WEEK:

1.

2.

3.

MAR

2014

3

4

5

NOTES

MAR
2014

6

7

8

9

MUST-DO THIS WEEK:

1.

2.

3.

MAR

2014

10

11

12

NOTES

MAR
2014

13

14

15

16

MUST-DO THIS WEEK:

1.

2.

3.

MAR

2014

17

18

19

NOTES

MAR

2014

20

21

22

23

MUST-DO THIS WEEK:

1.

2.

3.

MAR

2014

24

25

26

NOTES

MAR
2014

27

28

29

30

TO ACCOMPLISH IN ...

APRIL

1
2
3
4
5
6
7
8
9
10
11
12
13
14
15
16
17
18
19
20
21
22
23
24
25
26
27
28
29
30

❧ LIVE FREE : LOVE LIFE ❧

MAY

1
2
3
4
5
6
7
8
9
10
11
12
13
14
15
16
17
18
19
20
21
22
23
24
25
26
27
28
29
30
31

❧ LIVE FREE : LOVE LIFE ❧

2014

TO ACCOMPLISH IN ...

JUNE

1
2
3
4
5
6
7
8
9
10
11
12
13
14
15
16
17
18
19
20
21
22
23
24
25
26
27
28
29
30

LIVE FREE : LOVE LIFE

2014

NOTES

LIVE FREE : LOVE LIFE

APRIL 2014

SUNDAY	MONDAY	TUESDAY	WEDNESDAY	THURSDAY	FRIDAY	SATURDAY
		1	2	3	4	5
6	7	8	9	10	11	12
13	14	15	16	17	18	19
20	21	22	23	24	25	26
27	28	29	30			

MARCH 2014
S	M	T	W	T	F	S
						1
2	3	4	5	6	7	8
9	10	11	12	13	14	15
16	17	18	19	20	21	22
23	24	25	26	27	28	29

MAY 2014
S	M	T	W	T	F	S
				1	2	3
4	5	6	7	8	9	10
11	12	13	14	15	16	17
18	19	20	21	22	23	24
25	26	27	28	29	30	31

NOTES:

TO-DO IN ...   APRIL

MUST-DO THIS WEEK:

1.

2.

3.

APR

2014

31

MAR

1

2

NOTES

APR
2014

3

4

5

6

MUST-DO THIS WEEK:

1.

2.

3.

APR

2014

7

8

9

NOTES

APR

2014

10

11

12

13

MUST-DO THIS WEEK:

1.

2.

3.

APR

2014

14

15

16

NOTES

APR

2014

17

18

19

20

MUST-DO THIS WEEK:

1.
2.
3.

APR

2014

21

22

23

NOTES

APR

2014

24

25

26

27

MUST-DO THIS WEEK:

1.

2.

3.

APR

2014

28

29

30

NOTES

1	
MAY	
2	
3	
4	

 MAY 2014

SUNDAY	MONDAY	TUESDAY	WEDNESDAY	THURSDAY	FRIDAY	SATURDAY
APRIL 2014 / JUNE 2014				1	2	3
4	5	6	7	8	9	10
11	12	13	14	15	16	17
18	19	20	21	22	23	24
25	26	27	28	29	30	31

APRIL 2014

S	M	T	W	T	F	S
		1	2	3	4	5
6	7	8	9	10	11	12
13	14	15	16	17	18	19
20	21	22	23	24	25	26
27	28	29	30			

JUNE 2014

S	M	T	W	T	F	S
1	2	3	4	5	6	7
8	9	10	11	12	13	14
15	16	17	18	19	20	21
22	23	24	25	26	27	28
29	30					

NOTES:

TO-DO IN ...   MAY

MUST-DO THIS WEEK:

1.

2.

3.

MAY

2014

5

6

7

NOTES

MAY

2014

8

9

10

11

MUST-DO THIS WEEK:

1.

2.

3.

MAY

2014

12

13

14

NOTES

MAY

2014

15

16

17

18

MUST-DO THIS WEEK:

1.

2.

3.

MAY

2014

19

20

21

NOTES

MAY

2014

22

23

24

25

MUST-DO THIS WEEK:

1.

2.

3.

MAY

2014

26

27

28

NOTES

MAY

2014

29

30

31

1

JUNE

JUNE 2014

SUNDAY	MONDAY	TUESDAY	WEDNESDAY	THURSDAY	FRIDAY	SATURDAY
1	2	3	4	5	6	7
8	9	10	11	12	13	14
15	16	17	18	19	20	21
22	23	24	25	26	27	28
29	30					

MAY 2014

S	M	T	W	T	F	S
				1	2	3
4	5	6	7	8	9	10
11	12	13	14	15	16	17
18	19	20	21	22	23	24
25	26	27	28	29	30	31

JULY 2014

S	M	T	W	T	F	S
		1	2	3	4	5
6	7	8	9	10	11	12
13	14	15	16	17	18	19
20	21	22	23	24	25	26
27	28	29	30	31		

NOTES:

TO-DO IN ... JUNE

MUST-DO THIS WEEK:

1.

2.

3.

JUN

2014

2

3

4

NOTES

JUN

2014

5

6

7

8

MUST-DO THIS WEEK:

1.

2.

3.

JUN

2014

9

10

11

NOTES

JUN

2014

12

13

14

15

MUST-DO THIS WEEK:

1.

2.

3.

JUN

2014

16

17

18

NOTES

JUN
2014

19

20

21

22

MUST-DO THIS WEEK:

1.

2.

3.

JUN

2014

23

24

25

NOTES

JUN

2014

26

27

28

29

MID-YEAR REVIEW

What feels good about the first half of 2014? What's clicking?

What areas of your life or business are feeling out of sync?

What do you want the rest of the year to feel like? What would you like to see take shape?

What will you need to do to make that visualization come true?

What would you like to stop doing? What's eating up your time, making you feel bad, or not contributing to your best life in any way?

WHAT'S WORKING?

What activities, products, actions, or ideas are working for you this year?

What was your best creative business payday? What product or services are selling well? What actions bring subscribers, fans and followers?

(If there are none, don't worry! But take note. Going forward, you'll want to focus your efforts on activities that DO generate these results.)

What isn't working? What's costing time and money without generating a return?

What do you want MORE of in the second-half of 2014?

How might you change your approach going forward?

TO ACCOMPLISH IN ...

JULY

1
2
3
4
5
6
7
8
9
10
11
12
13
14
15
16
17
18
19
20
21
22
23
24
25
26
27
28
29
30
31

❧LIVE FREE : LOVE LIFE❧

AUGUST

1
2
3
4
5
6
7
8
9
10
11
12
13
14
15
16
17
18
19
20
21
22
23
24
25
26
27
28
29
30
31

❧LIVE FREE : LOVE LIFE❧

2014

TO ACCOMPLISH IN ...

SEPTEMBER

1
2
3
4
5
6
7
8
9
10
11
12
13
14
15
16
17
18
19
20
21
22
23
24
25
26
27
28
29
30

❧ LIVE FREE : LOVE LIFE ❧

2 0 1 4

NOTES

❧ LIVE FREE : LOVE LIFE ❧

JULY 2014

SUNDAY	MONDAY	TUESDAY	WEDNESDAY	THURSDAY	FRIDAY	SATURDAY
		1	2	3	4	5
6	7	8	9	10	11	12
13	14	15	16	17	18	19
20	21	22	23	24	25	26
27	28	29	30	31		

JUNE 2014
S M T W T F S
1 2 3 4 5 6 7
8 9 10 11 12 13 14
15 16 17 18 19 20 21
22 23 24 25 26 27 28
29 30

AUGUST 2014
S M T W T F S
1 2
3 4 5 6 7 8 9
10 11 12 13 14 15 16
17 18 19 20 21 22 23
24 25 26 27 28 29 30

NOTES:

TO-DO IN ...   JULY

MUST-DO THIS WEEK:

1.
2.
3.

JUL

2014

30

JUN

1

2

NOTES

JUL

2014

3

4

5

6

MUST-DO THIS WEEK:

1.

2.

3.

JUL

2014

7

8

9

NOTES

JUL

2014

10

11

12

13

MUST-DO THIS WEEK:

1.

2.

3.

JUL
2014

14

15

16

NOTES

JUL

2014

17

18

19

20

MUST-DO THIS WEEK:

1.

2.

3.

JUL

2014

21

22

23

NOTES

JUL

2014

24

25

26

27

MUST-DO THIS WEEK:

1.

2.

3.

JUL

2014

28

29

30

NOTES

JUL

2014

31

AUG

1

2

3

AUGUST 2014

SUNDAY	MONDAY	TUESDAY	WEDNESDAY	THURSDAY	FRIDAY	SATURDAY
JULY 2014 / SEPTEMBER 2014					1	2
3	4	5	6	7	8	9
10	11	12	13	14	15	16
17	18	19	20	21	22	23
24 / 31	25	26	27	28	29	30

JULY 2014

S	M	T	W	T	F	S
		1	2	3	4	5
6	7	8	9	10	11	12
13	14	15	16	17	18	19
20	21	22	23	24	25	26
27	28	29	30	31		

SEPTEMBER 2014

S	M	T	W	T	F	S
	1	2	3	4	5	6
7	8	9	10	11	12	13
14	15	16	17	18	19	20
21	22	23	24	25	26	27
28	29	30				

NOTES:

TO-DO IN ... AUGUST

MUST-DO THIS WEEK:

1.

2.

3.

AUG

2014

4

5

6

NOTES

AUG
2014

7

8

9

10

MUST-DO THIS WEEK:

1.

2.

3.

AUG

2014

11

12

13

NOTES

AUG

2014

14

15

16

17

MUST-DO THIS WEEK:

1.

2.

3.

AUG

2014

18

19

20

NOTES

AUG

2014

21

22

23

24

MUST-DO THIS WEEK:

1.

2.

3.

AUG
2014

25

26

27

NOTES

AUG

2014

28

29

30

31

SEPTEMBER 2014

SUNDAY	MONDAY	TUESDAY	WEDNESDAY	THURSDAY	FRIDAY	SATURDAY
	1	2	3	4	5	6
7	8	9	10	11	12	13
14	15	16	17	18	19	20
21	22	23	24	25	26	27
28	29	30				

AUGUST 2014

S	M	T	W	T	F	S
					1	2
3	4	5	6	7	8	9
10	11	12	13	14	15	16
17	18	19	20	21	22	23
24	25	26	27	28	29	30

OCTOBER 2014

S	M	T	W	T	F	S
			1	2	3	4
5	6	7	8	9	10	11
12	13	14	15	16	17	18
19	20	21	22	23	24	25
26	27	28	29	30	31	

NOTES:

TO-DO IN ... SEPTEMBER

MUST-DO THIS WEEK:

1.

2.

3.

SEP

2014

1

2

3

NOTES

SEP

2014

4

5

6

7

MUST-DO THIS WEEK:

1.

2.

3.

SEP

2014

8

9

10

NOTES

SEP

2014

11

12

13

14

MUST-DO THIS WEEK:

1.
2.
3.

SEP

2014

15

16

17

NOTES

SEP

2014

18

19

20

21

MUST-DO THIS WEEK:

1.

2.

3.

SEP

2014

22

23

24

NOTES

SEP

2014

25

26

27

28

15 BEFORE 2015

Before you launch into creating your 15 Before 2015 (15 goals you want to accomplish BEFORE the New Year), look back over your list of 25 goals and top 5 intentions.

What do you need to clear out of the way before the New Year?

What unfinished business do you need to attend to so that you can start the New Year with a clean slate?

What do you need to research or learn before making your goals happen?

What projects do you have to let go of? What commitments might you need to say "no" to?

What people, activities, and events do you want to really enjoy and be present for during this time?

15 BEFORE 2015

1.

2.

3.

4.

5.

6.

7.

8.

9.

10.

11.

12.

13.

14.

15.

TO ACCOMPLISH IN...

OCTOBER

1
2
3
4
5
6
7
8
9
10
11
12
13
14
15
16
17
18
19
20
21
22
23
24
25
26
27
28
29
30
31

❧LIVE FREE : LOVE LIFE❧

NOVEMBER

1
2
3
4
5
6
7
8
9
10
11
12
13
14
15
16
17
18
19
20
21
22
23
24
25
26
27
28
29
30

❧LIVE FREE : LOVE LIFE❧

2014

TO ACCOMPLISH IN ...

DECEMBER

1
2
3
4
5
6
7
8
9
10
11
12
13
14
15
16
17
18
19
20
21
22
23
24
25
26
27
28
29
30
31

❧ LIVE FREE : LOVE LIFE ❧

2014

NOTES

❧ LIVE FREE : LOVE LIFE ❧

OCTOBER 2014

SUNDAY	MONDAY	TUESDAY	WEDNESDAY	THURSDAY	FRIDAY	SATURDAY
SEPTEMBER 2014 / NOVEMBER 2014				1	2	3	4
5	6	7	8	9	10	11
12	13	14	15	16	17	18
19	20	21	22	23	24	25
26	27	28	29	30	31	

SEPTEMBER 2014

S	M	T	W	T	F	S
	1	2	3	4	5	6
7	8	9	10	11	12	13
14	15	16	17	18	19	20
21	22	23	24	25	26	27
28	29	30				

NOVEMBER 2014

S	M	T	W	T	F	S
						1
2	3	4	5	6	7	8
9	10	11	12	13	14	15
16	17	18	19	20	21	22
23	24	25	26	27	28	29

NOTES:

TO-DO IN ... OCTOBER

MUST-DO THIS WEEK:

1.

2.

3.

OCT

2014

29

SEPT

30

1

NOTES

OCT

2014

2

3

4

5

MUST-DO THIS WEEK:

1.

2.

3.

OCT

2014

6

7

8

NOTES

OCT
2014

9

10

11

12

MUST-DO THIS WEEK:

1.

2.

3.

OCT

2014

13

14

15

NOTES

OCT

2014

16

17

18

19

MUST-DO THIS WEEK:

1.

2.

3.

OCT

2014

20

21

22

NOTES

OCT

2014

23

24

25

26

	MUST-DO THIS WEEK:
	1.
	2.
	3.

OCT

2014

27	
28	
29	
NOTES	

OCT

2014

30

31

NOV

1

2

NOVEMBER 2014

SUNDAY	MONDAY	TUESDAY	WEDNESDAY	THURSDAY	FRIDAY	SATURDAY
OCTOBER 2014 / DECEMBER 2014						1
2	3	4	5	6	7	8
9	10	11	12	13	14	15
16	17	18	19	20	21	22
23 / 30	24	25	26	27	28	29

OCTOBER 2014

S	M	T	W	T	F	S
			1	2	3	4
5	6	7	8	9	10	11
12	13	14	15	16	17	18
19	20	21	22	23	24	25
26	27	28	29	30	31	

DECEMBER 2014

S	M	T	W	T	F	S
	1	2	3	4	5	6
7	8	9	10	11	12	13
14	15	16	17	18	19	20
21	22	23	24	25	26	27
28	29	30	31			

NOTES:

TO-DO IN ... NOVEMBER

MUST-DO THIS WEEK:

1.

2.

3.

NOV

2014

3

4

5

NOTES

NOV
2014

6

7

8

9

MUST-DO THIS WEEK:

1.

2.

3.

NOV

2014

10

11

12

NOTES

NOV

2014

13

14

15

16

MUST-DO THIS WEEK:

1.

2.

3.

NOV

2014

17

18

19

NOTES

NOV

2014

20

21

22

23

MUST-DO THIS WEEK:

1.

2.

3.

NOV

2014

24

25

26

NOTES

NOV
2014

27

28

29

30

DECEMBER 2014

SUNDAY	MONDAY	TUESDAY	WEDNESDAY	THURSDAY	FRIDAY	SATURDAY
	1	2	3	4	5	6
7	8	9	10	11	12	13
14	15	16	17	18	19	20
21	22	23	24	25	26	27
28	29	30	31			

NOVEMBER 2014

S	M	T	W	T	F	S
						1
2	3	4	5	6	7	8
9	10	11	12	13	14	15
16	17	18	19	20	21	22
23	24	25	26	27	28	29

JANUARY 2015

S	M	T	W	T	F	S
				1	2	3
4	5	6	7	8	9	10
11	12	13	14	15	16	17
18	19	20	21	22	23	24
25	26	27	28	29	30	31

NOTES:

TO-DO IN ... DECEMBER

MUST-DO THIS WEEK:

1.

2.

3.

DEC

2014

NOTES

DEC

2014

4

5

6

7

MUST-DO THIS WEEK:

1.

2.

3.

DEC

2014

8

9

10

NOTES

DEC

2014

11

12

13

14

MUST-DO THIS WEEK:

1.

2.

3.

DEC

2014

15

16

17

NOTES

DEC

2014

18

19

20

21

MUST-DO THIS WEEK:

1.

2.

3.

DEC

2014

22

23

24

NOTES

DEC

2014

25

26

27

28

MUST-DO THIS WEEK:

1.

2.

3.

DEC

2014

29

30

31

NOTES

JAN

2015

1

2

3

4

NOTES

NOTES

❧ NOTES ☙

Made in the USA
Lexington, KY
16 February 2014